MW01118952

In Loving Memories Of

_____

Born   / /   – Date   / /

Life
Has To End.
Love Doesn't.

HARKATI DESIGNS

POWERED BY AMZ

A humble request...

Dear Valued Customer,

We are a small, family-owned publishing company and without your support, we would not exist.

Therefore, we make a humble request - if you enjoy this book, please spare a few minutes to leave us a review on this book Amazon Product Page.

Each one of your reviews is paramount to our survival and helps us to compete against larger corporations with bigger marketing budgets that we don't have.

We are forever grateful For your support and we hope we have succeeded in providing you a very special book.

Sincerely,

Harkati Family

Name	Thoughts & Memories

Name

Thoughts & Memories

Name	Thoughts & Memories

Name

Thoughts & Memories

Name

Thoughts & Memories

_____

_____

_____

_____

_____

_____

_____

Name

Thoughts & Memories

Name

Thoughts & Memories

Name

Thoughts & Memories

Name

Thoughts & Memories

Name	Thoughts & Memories

Name

Thoughts & Memories

Name

_____

_____

_____

_____

_____

_____

Thoughts & Memories

_____

_____

_____

_____

_____

_____

_____

_____

_____

_____

_____

Name

Thoughts & Memories

Name

Thoughts & Memories

Name

Thoughts & Memories

Name

Thoughts & Memories

Name

_____

_____

_____

_____

_____

Thoughts & Memories

_____

_____

_____

_____

_____

_____

_____

_____

_____

_____

Name

Thoughts & Memories

Name

_____

_____

_____

_____

_____

_____

Thoughts & Memories

_____

_____

_____

_____

_____

_____

_____

_____

_____

_____

_____

Name

Thoughts & Memories

Name

Thoughts & Memories

Name	Thoughts & Memories

Name

Thoughts & Memories

Name   Thoughts & Memories

_____   _____

_____   _____

_____   _____

_____   _____

_____   _____

_____   _____

_____   _____

                                  _____

Name

Thoughts & Memories

Name

Thoughts & Memories

Name

Thoughts & Memories

Name	Thoughts & Memories

Name	Thoughts & Memories

Name

Thoughts & Memories

Name	Thoughts & Memories

Name	Thoughts & Memories

Name

Thoughts & Memories

Name

Thoughts & Memories

Name

Thoughts & Memories

Name

Thoughts & Memories

_____

_____

_____

_____

_____

_____

_____

_____

_____

_____

_____

_____

_____

_____

_____

_____

_____

_____

Name

Thoughts & Memories

Name

Thoughts & Memories

Name

Thoughts & Memories

Name

Thoughts & Memories

Name

Thoughts & Memories

Name

_____

_____

_____

_____

_____

_____

Thoughts & Memories

_____

_____

_____

_____

_____

_____

_____

_____

_____

_____

_____

_____

Name	Thoughts & Memories

Name

Thoughts & Memories

Name

Thoughts & Memories

Name

Thoughts & Memories

Name | Thoughts & Memories

Name

Thoughts & Memories

Name

Thoughts & Memories

Name

Thoughts & Memories

Name

Thoughts & Memories

Name

Thoughts & Memories

Name

Thoughts & Memories

Name

Thoughts & Memories

Name

Thoughts & Memories

Name

_____

_____

_____

_____

_____

_____

Thoughts & Memories

_____

_____

_____

_____

_____

_____

_____

_____

_____

_____

_____

Name

Thoughts & Memories

Name

Thoughts & Memories

Name

Thoughts & Memories

Name

| Thoughts & Memories

Name

Thoughts & Memories

_____

_____

_____

_____

_____

_____

_____

Name

Thoughts & Memories

Name

_____

_____

_____

_____

_____

_____

_____

Thoughts & Memories

_____

_____

_____

_____

_____

_____

_____

_____

_____

_____

_____

Name

Thoughts & Memories

Name

Thoughts & Memories

Name

Thoughts & Memories

_____

_____

_____

_____

_____

_____

_____

Name

Thoughts & Memories

Name	Thoughts & Memories

Name

Thoughts & Memories

Name

Thoughts & Memories

Name

Thoughts & Memories

_____

_____

_____

_____

_____

_____

_____

Name

Thoughts & Memories

Name

Thoughts & Memories

Name

Thoughts & Memories

Name

Thoughts & Memories

Name

Thoughts & Memories

Name

Thoughts & Memories

Name

Thoughts & Memories

Name

Thoughts & Memories

Name

| Thoughts & Memories

Name

Thoughts & Memories

Name

Thoughts & Memories

Name

Thoughts & Memories

Name

Thoughts & Memories

Name

Thoughts & Memories

Name

Thoughts & Memories

Name

Thoughts & Memories

Name

Thoughts & Memories

Name

Thoughts & Memories

Name

Thoughts & Memories

Name

_____

_____

_____

_____

_____

Thoughts & Memories

_____

_____

_____

_____

_____

_____

_____

_____

_____

_____

Name | Thoughts & Memories

Name

Thoughts & Memories

Name

Thoughts & Memories

Name	Thoughts & Memories

Name

| Thoughts & Memories

_____

_____

_____

_____

_____

_____

Name

Thoughts & Memories

Name

Thoughts & Memories

Name

_____

_____

_____

_____

_____

_____

Thoughts & Memories

_____

_____

_____

_____

_____

_____

_____

_____

_____

_____

_____

Name

Thoughts & Memories

Name	Thoughts & Memories

Name

Thoughts & Memories

Name

Thoughts & Memories

Name

Thoughts & Memories

Name

Thoughts & Memories

Name

Thoughts & Memories

Name

Thoughts & Memories

Name

_____

_____

_____

_____

_____

_____

Thoughts & Memories

_____

_____

_____

_____

_____

_____

_____

_____

_____

_____

Name

Thoughts & Memories

Name	Thoughts & Memories

Name

Thoughts & Memories

Name

Thoughts & Memories

Name | Thoughts & Memories

Name

Thoughts & Memories

Name	Thoughts & Memories

Name

Thoughts & Memories

Made in the USA
Las Vegas, NV
15 April 2025

20977185R00072